# London

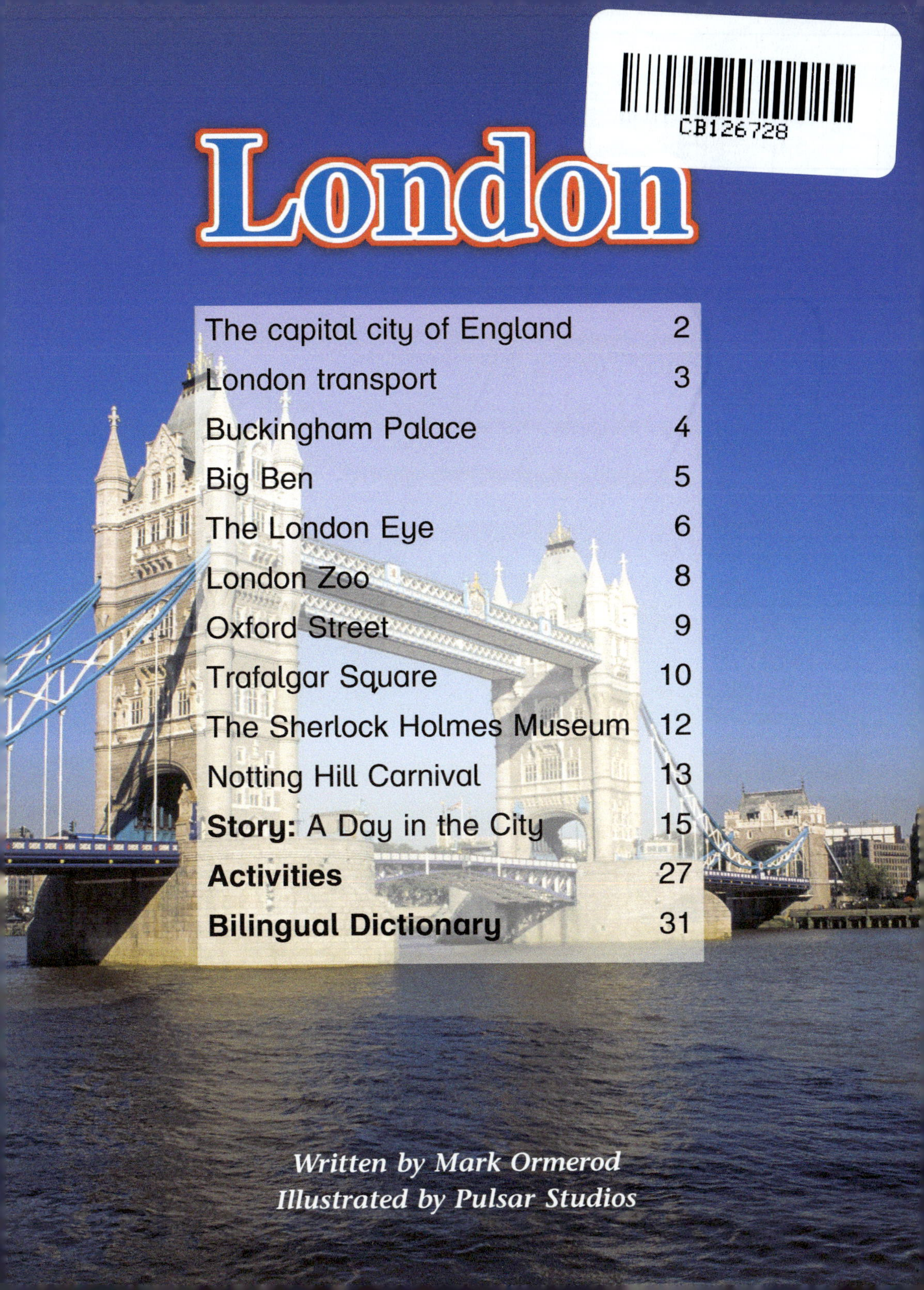




*Written by Mark Ormerod*
*Illustrated by Pulsar Studios*

# The capital city of England

London is the capital city of England. It is in the south-east of England, on the River Thames.

More than seven million people live in London and millions of tourists visit the city every year. London is bigger than all the other cities in the UK.

## London transport

London is very big, so you can't walk everywhere. People travel by car, bike, motorbike, bus or taxi. There are lots of red double-decker buses and black taxis in the streets of London.

Many people travel on the London underground. Parts of the London underground are very old. It was the first underground system in the world. Today, it has got twelve different lines and more than 275 stations.

## Buckingham Palace

This is Buckingham Palace. The King lives here when he is in London. The palace has got 600 rooms but the King only lives in twelve of them.

Many guards protect the palace. They are famous for the hats they wear. At half past eleven every day, you can watch a ceremony called 'The Changing of the Guard'.

## Big Ben

This is Big Ben. The tower is 96 metres tall. The clock has got four faces, so you can see the time from all directions.

Everyone calls the clock 'Big Ben'. The name refers to the bell inside the clock. You can hear the bell every hour.

## The London Eye

This is the London Eye. It's an enormous observation wheel next to the River Thames. It's 135 metres tall.

People go on the London Eye to see the incredible views of London. The wheel takes 30 minutes to turn 360°.

From the top of the London Eye, you can see views of the city in all directions. On a clear day, you can see for 40 kilometres. You can see the River Thames, Big Ben, the garden in Buckingham Palace and London Zoo.

# London Zoo

London Zoo has got more than 12,000 animals, including this Asian lion. In the past, the animals were in cages but now they live in spaces similar to their natural habitats.

An Asian lion

London Zoo was the first zoo to open a reptile house in 1849. The reptile house appears in the film *Harry Potter and the Philosopher's Stone*, when Harry talks to a snake.

# Oxford Street

This is Oxford Street. The street is more than two kilometres long and has got more than 300 shops. Here you can buy clothes, shoes, CDs, DVDs, computer games, books, earrings, postcards and souvenirs of London.

In December, there are lots of decorations and Christmas lights in Oxford Street.

## Trafalgar Square

This is Trafalgar Square. The name of the square comes from a famous battle in 1805. The man at the top of the column was a captain in the battle. His name was Horatio Nelson. The column is 52 metres tall.

Nelson's Column

This is the National Gallery. Here you can see very famous paintings by Pablo Picasso, Leonardo da Vinci and other artists.

In December, you can see an enormous Christmas tree in Trafalgar Square. The tree comes from Norway. It is a symbol of friendship between the people of Norway and Britain. On 31st December, lots of people stand in the square to hear Big Ben at midnight. It's an exciting start to the New Year.

## The Sherlock Holmes Museum

Welcome to 221b Baker Street. This was the house of the famous detective, Sherlock Holmes. The house is now a museum. Here you can see Sherlock's violin, his notebook and his famous hat.

You can read about the cases of Sherlock Holmes. There are eight Sherlock Holmes books and many short stories.

## Notting Hill Carnival

Notting Hill is an area of London. For three days in the summer, people come to Notting Hill to celebrate the Carnival. They sing and dance in the street. They play music and wear colourful costumes.

People from many different cultures live in London. The Notting Hill Carnival is a celebration of this cultural diversity.

In London, there are more than 40,000 shops. There are more than 80 markets. There are more than 130 theatres and more than 100 museums. There are more than 140 parks.

You can't be bored in London. There's lots to see and do.

# A Day in the City

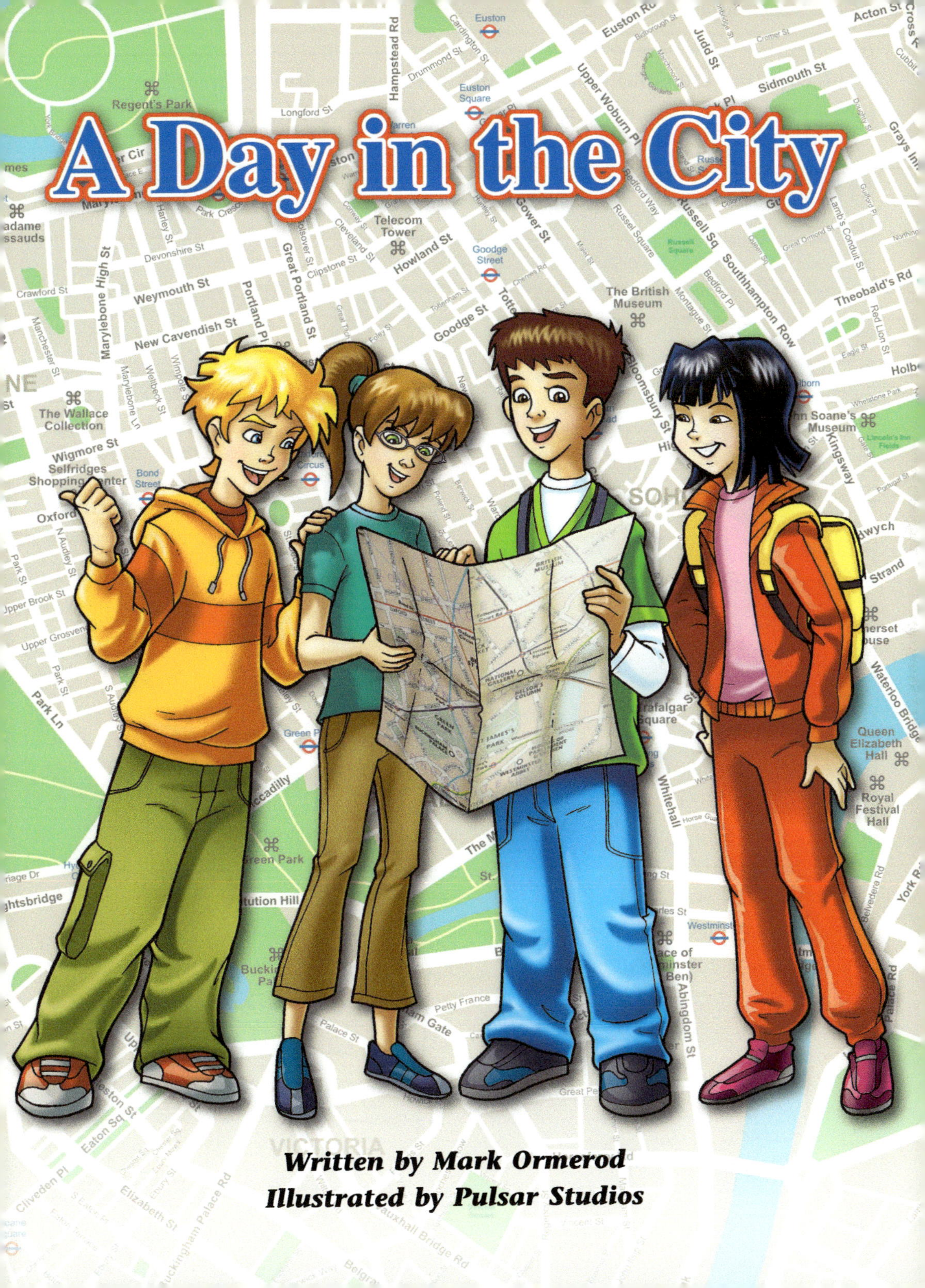


**Written by Mark Ormerod**
**Illustrated by Pulsar Studios**

Tim, Clare, Kate and Phil are in Hyde Park, in the centre of London. Tim is reading a book about the city. Kate and Phil are eating sandwiches. Clare is writing a postcard to a friend.

Suddenly, there are lots of photographers in the park. They are running very quickly.
Sorry!
Hey!
What's happening? Is there a famous person in the park?

Phil talks to two of the photographers.
The Prime Minister is planting a tree.
We're taking photographs for the newspapers.

Later, in the afternoon, the children look at the tree.
Look! Here's a wallet.
Look inside. Is there a telephone number? You can call the owner on your mobile phone.

Tim looks in the wallet.
This wallet belongs to the Prime Minister!
No problem! We can take it to his house. Where does the Prime Minister live?

Tim looks for information about the Prime Minister's house in his guide book.

Outside the Prime Minister's house, the children talk to two policemen.

The children travel to Wimbledon on the underground.
This book says that Wimbledon is a very famous Tennis Club. It's got 28 grass courts. Every tennis player in the world wants to play in the final of the Wimbledon tournament.
FIND OUT ABOUT LONDON
Centre Court, Wimbledon.

At Wimbledon, outside centre court, the children speak to a very tall security guard.
T BLACK 3 6 15
CENTRE COURT
I'm sorry. You can't see the Prime Minister. He's watching the tennis final. But you can give his wallet to me. And then I can give it to the Prime Minister.
No, I'm sorry. We can't give the wallet to you.
No problem! We can wait for the Prime Minister here.
EXIT
CAFE

The children wait outside centre court. They watch the tennis match on an enormous screen.

The children eat strawberries and cream.

After three hours, the tennis match finishes and the Prime Minister leaves centre court. When Kate, Tim, Clare and Phil give the Prime Minister his wallet, the photographers take lots of photos.

The children travel to the Prime Minister's house in his car. They talk about their school, their families and their friends. And the Prime Minister talks about his school, his family and his friends.

The Prime Minister and the children continue their conversation at his house. They have tea and biscuits, and they talk about many different things.

The next day, there are photos of Clare, Tim, Kate and Phil in all the newspapers.
THE NEWS
FOUR VERY HONEST CHILDREN
THE TIME
CHILDREN RETURN THE PRIME MINISTER'S WALLET
THE WORLD
CHILDREN HAVE TEA WITH THE PRIME MINISTER

And a week later, when the children are back at school, they receive a letter from the Prime Minister.
May 2007
Dear Phil, Clare, Tim and Kate
I want to thank you again for returning my wallet. It was very kind and very honest of you.
It was a pleasure to meet you. I was very interested to hear about the magazine you write at school. Please send me a copy.
Best wishes
THE PRIME MINISTER

# Activities

## 1 Find these words in the word puzzle. Complete the sentence.

| a | r | p | g | u | f | b | l | b | u | r |
|---|---|---|---|---|---|---|---|---|---|---|
| u | n | d | e | r | g | r | o | u | n | d |
| m | p | l | e | e | o | g | m | s | d | s |
| b | b | i | k | e | e | t | v | c | e | a |
| u | a | c | m | l | k | a | r | c | a | r |
| n | s | s | o | r | w | x | k | l | g | a |
| m | o | t | o | r | b | i | k | e | r | o |

People in London travel by b i k e, by double-decker

_ _ _, by _ _ _ _, by _ _ _ _ _ _ _ _ _,

by _ _ _ or on the _ _ _ _ _ _ _ _ _ _ _.

## 2 Answer the questions.

Buckingham Palace ~~The London Eye~~ Oxford Street
The National Gallery Big Ben Notting Hill
London Zoo Trafalgar Square

1 Where can you see views of London? The London Eye
2 Where can you buy clothes, CDs and souvenirs? ______
3 Where can you see famous paintings? ______
4 Where can you see a Christmas tree in December? ______
5 Where can you see an Asian lion? ______
6 Where can you see a carnival in summer? ______
7 Where can you see the time? ______
8 Where can you see 'The Changing of the Guard'? ______

## 3 Read and complete.

1 London is on the River ___Thames___ . sTeham

2 The King lives at Buckingham ______________ . caPale

3 Nelson's Column is in Trafalgar ______________ . quaSer

4 The Sherlock Holmes ______________ is in Baker Street. suuMem

5 There are more than 12,000 animals in London ______________ . oZo

6 There are lots of shops in Oxford ______________ . eStret

7 There are famous paintings in the National ______________ . reGally

## 4 Find and write the answers.

1 How tall is Big Ben?

Big Ben is 96 metres tall.

2 How tall is the London Eye?

______________

3 How tall is Nelson's Column?

______________

## 5 Circle T (True) or F (False).

1 The London Eye is shorter than Nelson's Column. T (F)

2 Nelson's Column is taller than Big Ben. T F

3 The London Eye is shorter than Big Ben. T F

4 Big Ben is shorter than the London Eye. T F

5 The London Eye is taller than Nelson's Column and Big Ben. T F

## 6 Write the words.

1

2

3

1 guard

4

5

6

7

## 7 Number the sentences in the correct order.

- [ ] The children go to Wimbledon on the underground.
- [ ] The Prime Minister sends them a letter to say thank you.
- [ ] The children see the Prime Minister plant a tree.
- [ ] The children go to the Prime Minister's house for tea.
- [1] The children are in Hyde Park having a picnic.
- [ ] The children find the Prime Minister's wallet.
- [ ] The children give the Prime Minister his wallet.

## 8 Who said what? Match the speech bubbles to the pictures.

a

b

c

d

e

f

1

1 Please come to my house for tea.

2 The Prime Minister isn't at home this afternoon.

3 But you can give his wallet to me.

4 No problem! We can wait for the Prime Minister here.

5 We're taking photographs for the newspapers.

6 I'm watching the tennis final.

# Bilingual Dictionary

Write the words in your language.

| | | | |
|---|---|---|---|
| at home | ______ | owner | ______ |
| battle | ______ | paintings | ______ |
| bell | ______ | palace | ______ |
| belong | ______ | park | ______ |
| between | ______ | photograph | ______ |
| biscuits | ______ | photographer | ______ |
| bored | ______ | pleasure | ______ |
| centre | ______ | postcard | ______ |
| city | ______ | Prime Minister | ______ |
| clock | ______ | river | ______ |
| conversation | ______ | souvenir | ______ |
| decorations | ______ | square | ______ |
| every hour | ______ | strawberries | ______ |
| every year | ______ | street | ______ |
| friendship | ______ | tennis match | ______ |
| gallery | ______ | tennis player | ______ |
| guard | ______ | theatre | ______ |
| honest | ______ | the underground | ______ |
| interested | ______ | tournament | ______ |
| interesting | ______ | transport | ______ |
| kind | ______ | United Kingdom (UK) | ______ |
| market | ______ | view | ______ |
| museum | ______ | wait | ______ |
| Norway | ______ | wallet | ______ |
| observation | ______ | wheel | ______ |

Macmillan Education
4 Crinan Street,
London N1 9XW
A division of Springer Nature Limited
Companies and representatives throughout the world

ISBN 978-1-3800-3775-6



First published 2007
This edition published in 2019



Illustrated by Pulsar Studios and Red Giraffe Limited
Designed by Red Giraffe Limited

The author and publishers would like to thank the following for permission to reproduce their photographs:

Cover Photography with the kind permission of Pictures Colour Library/Clive Sawyer.

Alamy/Jon Arnold Images pp1, 12, Alamy/Lourens Smak p3(t), Alamy Stock Photo/ Phillip Kraskoff p4(t), Alamy Stock Photo/Vishal Goenka p7, Alamy/PCL p9(t), Alamy/Elmtree Images p12(b), Alamy/Alex Segre p14(t), Alamy Stock photo/ Paul Thompson Images p14(b), Alamy Stock Photo/Imagedoc p21; Chris Dorney / Alamy Stock Photo p9(b); Corbis/David Ball p5, Corbis/Roger Tidman p8(t), FLPA/ZSSD/ Minden Pictures p8(b); Getty Images/Marvin E. Newman p7, Getty Images/ dikobraziy p15, Getty Images/iStock/_londongal_ p25, Getty Images/iStock/ andyparker72 p22, Getty Images/iStock/littleny p26, Getty Images/iStock/simonkr p27, Getty Images/iStock/lovemax p13, Getty Images/Light Rocket/SOPA Images p29; Image Source/MARS/James French p10; Robert Harding World Imagery/Walter Rowlings p6, Robert Harding/G. Richardson pp10-11, Robert Harding/Travel Library p11; Shutterstock/Matthew Ashmore p3(b), Shutterstock/Madison Muskopf p4(b).



Printed and bound in Brazil

2025
20